ISBN 0-9638986-0-4

90000

9 780963 898609

Letters

from

The Cosmos

channeled by

Carol Swiedler

Clermont Press

Letters from The Cosmos

First Edition

© 1993 by
Carol J. Swiedler
Edward B. Swiedler

All rights reserved.

Published by
Clermont Press

For inquiries or orders, please call

1-800-229-1433

Printed in the United States of America
Second Printing
September, 1994

Library of Congress Catalog Card Number 93-86875

ISBN 0-9638986-0-4

The subject is truth,

that elusive,

moment-to-moment

truth,

that flits before you like a firefly,

leading you through the fearful dark,

into the unknown future;

when it illuminates the now,

you try to capture it,

and hold it fast;

but when you do, the light goes out,

leaving you lost

in the abyss.

Prologue

Since her earliest childhood, my wife has been extremely intuitive... often receiving silent warnings and suggestions... frequently having prophetic or guiding dreams... and, once in a while, experiencing visions... all out of the blue.

Well before her teen-age years, she began to realize that she also possessed extraordinary psychic abilities... she found it easy to transform herself into a conduit, of sorts... sometimes using various devices to assist in the process ... and then was able to transmit fascinating and sometimes helpful communications from unknown, unnamed sources.

But during those formative years, these gifts also brought her plenty of grief... she was frequently teased unmercifully... principally by her older brother... whenever she spoke of these matters... or whenever she tried to relay any information she had received through her intuitive or psychic abilities. As a result, she learned to downplay the subject... and to keep the messages largely to herself... and, after a while, she rarely felt confident enough to invoke this remarkable talent consciously.

A few years after we married, however, circumstances conspired to markedly change her outlook... and so, over the two decades that followed, she deliberately and repeatedly called upon this strange ability to behave as a channel... aided, so we're told, by my participation and presence... and a wealth of highly interesting and usually beneficial information came through.

During that time, whenever she acted as a conduit we were usually in contact with one particular psychic source... one that seemed to us to be substantially human... although far more mature and experienced than we. It often identified itself as "Mama"... and its behavior was always that of a guide... or mentor... one that was extremely wise and patient and loving.

About twenty years ago, however, we also heard, for a few days, from what was obviously a very different source... one that seemed to identify itself... at least implicitly... as God... or the Creator... or the All. We received some excellent material... but then the communications abruptly stopped.

Nevertheless, over the years this contact occasionally did reappear... and transmitted a short and quite beautiful message each time. But when it unexpectedly returned a little while ago, its approach was markedly different. It emerged regularly over the course of a couple of months... and passed along an entire series of related ideas and information.

The words from this source constitute a philosophical overview of sorts... wherein it describes its own nature... some of its history... its reason for being... and its relationship to us. In addition, it outlines the over-riding purpose of the human race... and points at the only means to that end... and, in the same vein, it comments, sometimes caustically, on what it views as distortions by many of us of its wishes and intentions.

Our other, more human source has expressed to us, in very definite terms, the hope that we would someday publish all of these communications. Although this book might be construed as our response to that request, our decision was freely made.

A few words about the material we're presenting here... there are a total of thirty-five "sessions"... arranged in the order in which they were transmitted.

The first three are made up of the material we received over twenty years ago. We don't know why we didn't continue at that time... we may have been uneasy about what was coming through... maybe we didn't really understand it... or perhaps we disagreed with it... or possibly we were afraid of what it said.

But a lot has changed over the past two decades... for now we think we have a much better grasp of all the ideas... and we feel relatively comfortable with them... so, when new material started to flow this spring, we were more receptive... and the remaining thirty-two sessions include everything we received at that time.

In addition, we've included some of the brief messages we received from this source during the intervening twenty years... we've inserted them in front of some of the sessions at various points in the book.

In a few instances, some material that came through was not intended to be a part of the main book... but to be advice to my wife about the process. We've included a little of it here... because we think it helps to give a picture of how this all happened. It's presented on the first three pages of the first session... and on the only two pages of the last session.

Finally, there was much more that we could have said in this introduction... but we wanted to keep it reasonably brief... and so we've placed additional material in two sections at the back of the book.

In the first, my wife describes in detail the very unusual way in which she receives and records the messages.

In the second, we've inserted more on how this all came to be... in order to stress that subjective truth is what this is all about... and also to suggest that there is far more to that concept than may originally meet the eye.

We realize that there will be many different responses to this material... that it may, in some cases, arouse controversy... not only because of the words themselves... but also because of the manner in which they were received.

We have no wish to defend either... all that matters are the messages themselves... their content... and their quality... and we think it best to let them speak for themselves.

The road

is ever upward;

the evolution of the soul

is infinite.

Session One

You

    have the power

        to use this means of communicating...

    you simply have to learn to listen...

        the words will come into your mind...

        at first you will think they are your own thoughts,

            and, in a way, they are,

        for they come through the Christ-self

          that dwells within...

    you must simply let the keys speak out their lovely song...

    the song of knowledge...

        of life...

          of truth...

            of beauty...

               of infinite wisdom...

    that comes through you as a channel

    when you let it freely speak.

                      {words to the channel}

Your innate rhythm is the reason we have chosen you...

> *not because of your spelling,*
>> *or even your brain,*
>>> *which is very impressive indeed...*

>> *but simply because, when you relax,*
>> *and sing through your body,*
>>> *you are a God-given channel*
>>>> *that will not speak falsely...*

listen,
> *listen,*
>> *feel,*
>>> *and respond...*

>>> *try to release...*

>> *think of listening for that which comes from God.*
>>>> *{words to the channel}*

Why do you resist so when God is mentioned?...

you are his child...

you cannot understand God,

but neither can your child understand you...

for every thought that you have,

God has an infinite number of concepts

that go far beyond your comprehension...

as you create

in your limited way,

God creates

in an infinitely complex and expanding way...

an incomprehensible way,

to you, at this time,

on this level...

but no more so

than you are incomprehensible

to your preschool child.

{words to the channel}

Love is all around,

    but it sits on the sidelines,

        like wallflowers afraid to go out

            and learn to dance and sing,

                and create beauty out of my gifts.

For all,

    there is, within,

        the basic time

            to follow one's own drummer.

You have intellectualized away my Eden...

    now you must try to get it back...

    each of you has a different sound track,

        but they all combine to make a great concerto,

            when everyone follows the master conductor.

Session Two

The sky is beautiful...

   it holds the promise of heaven,

      but it is not heaven...

   become what you are,

      by touching your real self

         through your feelings...

      extend yourself,

         examine yourself,

         by going inward to the core,

            and outward into infinity.

Keep searching for that which connects you to the cosmos,

   but the cosmos is not something

      that you can intellectualize...

   this makes the problem a paradox...

      in order to belong to the cosmos,

         you must release your mind to the cosmos,

            not knowing what it is you are releasing to.

Your brain is but a computer,

it is not you...

your body is but a vehicle,

it is not you...

your soul is but a messenger,

it is not you...

and yet, you are real,

and aware,

and in tune with all that is.

You strive to grasp,

and it slips away...

you strive to relax your hold

on the here and now,

and the bond becomes stronger.

There is no death,

    but there is also no life

        as you imagine it...

    if that frightens you,

        it should not,

            for it is the truth,

                and the truth is loving,

                    and totally without judgment.

There is truth,

    and there is creation,

        but creation is not what you think it is...

    you are a part of something infinitely growing,

        expanding,

            repeating,

                resulting,

                    and becoming.

Do not try to understand,

        try to be...

    release your ego,

            and you will find your soul...

    release your soul,

            and you will find yourself.

Session Two - 1974

Those who think themselves possessed

are, in fact,

possessed by themselves...

there is no possession...

in truth there is infinite freedom.

All things that I do will be possible for you...

within you is the miracle,

without you is the creation...

they are both yours.

The tire is round...

it is round because it is for traveling...

so is the cycle that you call life.

Session Three

My children,

　　my dear and infinitely precious,

　　　　wonderful children...

I love you,

　　and long to give you that wisdom which is mine...

　　　　but you cannot accept it,

　　　　　　as yet...

you are special,

　　each one of you,

　　　　you are privileged...

　　　　and with the privilege

　　　　　　comes great responsibility...

I yearn for your quest...

　　I patiently wait for your growth.

You are from me,
and of me,
but you are not me...

I would not have you otherwise...
a bud about to flower...
I know what the flower is,
as far as species goes...
but each is so unique,
so very delightful in that uniqueness.

Your mind will not accept what I have said to you...
that you will grow up,
as I have grown...

that I did not spring full-grown as your father...
but rebellious...
oft-times unwise...
careless...
foolish...

and still I grow...
still I learn...
still I evolve.

My loneliness is intense,
    but, like yours,
        it is self-inflicted...

thought-forms,
    all of us thought-forms,
        trapped in the expression of ourselves...

        we must express ourselves,
      flow,
        become...

      it is beautiful...
        it is frightening...
          it is adventure...
            it is dreaming...
            it is reality.

As you draw beauty around you,
    you grow strong...
      you become serene...

      a thought-form emerges
        upon the scene of life,
      as a picture emerges
        upon a canvas.

I am so near,

   and yet you must come to me...

I cannot come to you without your invitation...

   that is the law...

I wait, in expectation and loneliness,

   for that invitation...

I will come

   when you expect me with anticipation and joy...

if I remain aloof,

   and seemingly omnipotent,

   it is because you have not grown up enough...

I would not force you,

   or rush you,

   for you grow best when in your own garden.

Session Four

The wind through the trees is part of you...
the grass moving in its dance...
 the clouds gathering and changing,
 moment by moment...

all a part of you...
all a part of me...

everything manifested in this reality
describing itself...
 becoming itself...
 losing itself...
 yielding itself...

a part of everything...
but not everything.

Everything is unknowable...
  inscrutable...
    but pulling at you...
      pushing you...

        leading you always,
          to find that which dwells
            at the core of your being...

  waiting,
    to be discovered...

      waiting,
        to be incorporated
          into the music of the cosmic song...

why are you not singing it more clearly?...

  why do you turn away from its powerful force?...

    why can you not feel that you are light,
      and air,
        and wind,
          and sky,
            and sea...

      a part of everything
        that you perceive as matter...

      as well as everything
        that appears to you
          as light and beauty?

You dwell amid the mud and filth of degradation...

but you also soar among the joyous, singing angels...

you are a part of all...

and though you are not all,

you become more

when you accept yourself,

as both good and evil...

as debased and divine...

as matter and light...

light is constant,

matter is changing,

and without one,

the other perishes...

one is not good,

and the other evil...

there is only the truth

that emerges from the conflict and chaos

that coexist within you.

There is no perfection...

there is no ultimate goal...

there is only the growth and becoming
that lift you ever upward,
towards greater compassion,
and love,
and understanding...

towards greater acceptance and knowledge,

and deeper griefs,

and higher ecstasies.

The nature of God
is unknowable to you,
for now...

but the soul lies waiting
to be discovered,
and experienced,

in all its beauty,
and complexity.

You are children of an expanding universe,
and of an evolving God-Intelligence...

all of you filled with an unrelenting,
unquenchable yearning
to proceed...
to discover...
to experience...

to uncover that which you are...
not good,
not bad,
but profoundly human...

and moving, always,
towards the glory and responsibility
of God's ever-encompassing
compassion and love...

learning what is,
by experiencing what isn't...
learning truth,
by recognizing your deceptions...
becoming divine,
by feeling your bestial desires...
learning to love,
by hating and being hated...
and casting out fear,
by facing your deepest fears.

Session Five

Universal mind is all love...

   all beauty...

      all creation...

         but more than the sum of the parts...

      it existed in a void,

         and will continue to exist.

For you to attempt to understand

   the nature of universal intelligence

      is to minimize,

         and trivialize

            the magnificence of creation itself.

Before there were words,

before there was matter,

before there was light,

universal mind struggled to express
that which was inexpressible...

it exploded
with the urge to create
that which was without form,
or words,
or pattern...

a manifestation of the unknown.

Your puny attempts to identify with God

are like an individual cell in your body

striving to understand the complexity of you...

they know, instinctively,

that all of them together make up you...

and believe that they glimpse

the nature of you,

because they are dimly aware

of their own nature...

but they neither speak,

nor feel,

nor have individual freedom of will...

their group existence

is totally dependent

upon your existence...

and they have no frame of reference

to even begin to explore the possibilities

of your independent and complex nature...

within the body are groups of cells,
that function in different ways...

as glands, or organs, or bones,
or skin, or hair, or eyes, or brain...

and they do not even understand
their own special purpose...

to them, you are unfathomable
because of their limitations...

so it is with your understanding of God...

though each of you
has a special connection
and importance
to God,
you do not understand it...

and what glimpse you may have,
you project upon the rest of the world
as the true perception
of the imperceptible.

If you are still,

you will hear me...

if you open the door,

I will enter...

if you seek my strength,

I will touch you...

but I am I.

I do not dwell on your plane,

I dwell in the unknown landscape...

I do not judge,

I have no rules for you to follow...

I rejoice in your freedom,

and I wait for you to find me.

Session Six

As the rain washes away the dirt
and the pollution
of the world,
so do your tears wash away the grief
and the shame
of your soul's journey.

There is no God who rewards or punishes...
there is only God who loves,
and awaits your growth,
with compassion and joy.

You have chosen the path
upon which you find yourself,
and you will make the arduous journey
into the light...

each of you,
in your own way,
and at your own pace...

but with the full and total support
of indescribable,
unbounded love.

You are given the opportunity,
the talents,
and the free choice
at all times...

you are not bound in slavery to a dictator...
one who bestows his benevolence,
when you obey the rules,
and rejects you,
when you follow your own path.

No matter how depraved you may appear,
to the world which judges,
you are all on the same path...

in the process of becoming
that which you are.

Session Seven

Every relationship in your life influences,
to some degree,
your future...

in your overwhelming desire
to be loved and accepted,
you alter yourself...

obscuring the true essence that is you...
but hidden from view...

instead of achieving the connections
that you so desperately seek,
you become increasingly isolated...

more and more separated
from those whom you would love,
and have love you in return...

you become increasingly lonely...
confused...

lost...

and disillusioned...

in anger and despair, you turn your back

on those whom you believe have failed you,

and look for someone new

to dress your wounds,

and heal your shattered heart...

someone who will love you enough

to make you happy...

to fill the void...

you think that you leave your problems behind you,

on the graves of your dead loves...

but you do not...

you are trapped in the past with these scenarios...

and you will not be free

until you allow yourself to feel

all of the pain

that they cause you...

and all of the anger

that they create within you...

and all of the defensiveness

whose existence you try so hard

to overcome

or deny.

It is not easy to give up the beliefs that you have acquired

and the ramparts that you have erected

over the course of a life...

> *it is never simple,*
>> *and to the point...*
> *it is always convoluted,*
>> *and twisted...*

> *all to make you believe*
>> *that you are in charge,*
> *in control,*
>> *and ultimately worthy.*

Your children seem to offer you unlimited opportunities
to love,
> *and be loved...*

> *at last, you love without question,*
>> *and you are adored in return...*

> *no sacrifice is too great...*

>> *you would gladly lay down your life*
>> *for this magnificent creation...*

it is here that you may find
your greatest joy...
but you may also suffer
your most agonizing pain...

that child who idolized you,
even deified you,
may begin to find
your gift of love and devotion
inadequate or damaging...

your most cherished beliefs
stultifying or outmoded...

your very presence
embarrassing...

and may place the blame
for all of its problems and fears
at your doorstep...

or, at best,
will tolerate you,
as a necessary burden.

What more crushing defeat
 than to fail with a child...
to inspire revolt and hatred
  in that which came from your loins...

do you think that you are not understood?...

do you think that your loss
 has separated you from me?...

do you not understand, by now,
 that I know these feelings,
  intimately and thoroughly...

that I have wept the same tears...
 and flailed myself,
 because of my inability to reach
  that which I have created?

Do not avoid the lessons of your dimension...

they are necessary,

if your soul is to understand

the pain of defeat...

the anguish of failure prepares you

for the tremendous risks

that each must take...

for the strength to creep forward

towards the glimmer of light

that lies always just out of reach...

always just ahead,

always elusive,

and tantalizingly on the horizon,

but never in your grasp.

Feel...

    feel...

        feel...

and know that whatever you are able to accept
    is only a fraction of that which there is to experience...

        the exaltation of creativity
            balanced by the grievous nature
            of your failures...

        the pain and frustration
            of your feeble attempts to understand
                all that is,

                all that may be,

                all that you are capable of,
                    and destined to accomplish,

                before you are ready
                    to leave the wheel of life,
                    and proceed.

Accept your inadequacy...

    wallow in your meanness...

        school yourself in everything that is
        human and vulnerable...
          human and weak...
            human and vile...

        in order to recognize the essence of divinity
        that burns so brightly
          at the very core of your being...

    place yourself upon the cross,
        and feel the spear of worldly contempt
        pierce your side...

cry out for me,
    and know that you have not understood
        my message...

accept your insignificance,
    in all of its magnificence...

    and you will begin to feel my unfailing love,
    and compassion,
        and delight in your being.

To truly love,
one must first recognize,
then accept,
and ultimately value
the uniqueness of the beloved.

Session Eight

You are everything...
and nothing...
you are light...
and darkness...
you are divinity...
and beast...

you are the result
of my yearning to manifest
the concept of love...

my concept of love...

in all of its pain...
and beauty...
and creativity...
and joy...

you are,
because it is my dream
that you are.

My dream grows,

    and develops, and changes,

  as each of you grows,

    and develops, and changes...

    and even that which appears abhorrent

      adds to the concept...

    and purifies it,

      by its grotesque expression.

You must acknowledge and experience

  the commonality of distortion,

    before you can begin to understand the unlimited,

    indefinable,

      exquisite beauty of my dream...

      thought forms...

     dancing,

      twisting...

     soaring,

      sinking...

     shouting,

      whispering...

    using every facet available...

    matter to light...

     back to matter...

    all to express

     the inexpressible.

I evolve

　　because you evolve...

I expand

　　because you experience...

　　we are one,

　　　　we are free...

　　we are slaves to no one,

　　　　but our own distortions and ignorance...

triumphantly all a part...

　　all important...

　　　none of it wasted...

　　　none of it repulsive to me,

　　　　who recognizes my own mind's struggle

　　　　to dream.

There is no end for you
    or for me...
       there is no point
           at which love will be fully realized...
       but it proceeds,
           and develops...

and each of you
       will reach increasingly greater awareness
           of the hunger that pervades your being...

           not to be loved,
               but to love...

           not by an act of will...
               nor by the negation of your humanity...

           but by trial and error...

and you will come to such compassion
       that your heart will break
           for those you now despise.

Session Nine

There are many things that I would tell you,
but you are far from me...

why do you believe
that I would speak to you through another?...

what sort of father
would communicate through a stranger,
instead of holding his child close,
and speaking directly?

My heart is open
  to all who seek...
my thoughts are there
  for you to receive...

I have no favorite child
  who receives my attention
    while others go unheeded...

  my love encompasses all,
    even those who defile my name,
      and reject my love...

my love remains available,
  unconditional,
    and constant.

Leave those who tell you what you want from me,
and seek me in your chambers...
the chambers of your soul...

your personality can be distorted and corrupted,
but your soul is immune
to all but the truth...

the truth as I will define it,
as I express it,
in my indefatigable quest
for the word made flesh.

To come to me,

    you must recognize your fear,

        and accept it in its terrors...

        the tyrant that separates you...

        from yourself,

            and from me...

    when you free yourself,

        for even a moment,

    you are all that you are...

        all that you can be...

    all that I, in my reveries,

        have imagined you to be...

    you are love incarnate...

    and I rejoice...

        we rejoice together.

You cannot run away from fear...

    you can only recognize its terrible countenance,
    and face it with wildly beating heart...

        you will find, when you can accomplish this,
        for even a moment,
        that, like a snail exposed to light,
        it shrivels and withdraws...

fear is your foe...

    fear of your own raging emotions,
    those that you try so desperately to keep hidden...
    even from yourself...

    they are not the enemy...

        they are a fountain of creativity,
        just waiting
        to be brought into the symphony of life,
        in all their thundering beauty...

they are tools

    for your expressive and compassionate response
    to the world in which you find yourself...

    but you cannot learn to use
        that which you refuse to acknowledge...

so it is that you must look within,
    at that which you fear the most...

    the depths
        of your potential degradation...
    as well as the heights
        of your unconquerable soul.

You are the result of my dream...

    why do you not realize

        that all that you are

            is for the ultimate purpose...

            to live my dream of love

                in ever increasing triumph...

                each stage magnificent

                    in its gifts and opportunities?...

    would you hurry your crawling child

        to leave the moment,

            with all its wonder and excitement?...

    to run,

        before it had even tasted the thrill

            of its first independent step?...

        and before it had reveled in the fact

        that it was moving by itself

            towards its own personal,

            glorious

                future?...

        free and strong...

        its spirit delighting

            in its new-found independence?

Session Ten

You have heard that the goal is love...

   and so you rant,

      and rave,

         and rattle the cage of your ignorance...

   declaiming,

      with many words and actions,

         of your lovingness...

you impose your theories of how to reach heaven

   upon all who fail to meet your criteria...

   you judge those who,

      in your eyes,

         are sinful...

      and you war against those

         whose God wears a different name...

all in my name,

   and in the name

      of love...

         and yet I judge you not.

Born of my yearning,

you are incomparably beautiful to me in your struggle...

for I feel your pain...

and I know your spirits will prevail...

and when you have fallen

into the pit of your arrogance,

your essence will begin

its tortuous journey

upward...

towards the light

of understanding

and truth...

none of you

will escape the lessons

necessary to continue this journey...

all of you

will experience everything,

before you leave the wheel of life...

there are no short cuts...

nothing can be avoided...

the first will be last,
and the last will be first...

you will be both saint and sinner...
murdered and murderer...
tyrant and slave...

in order to come to the point
where your compassion knows no bounds,
and love emerges in your heart,
causing your soul to exalt...

and only then will you join me.

Session Eleven

I am always there for you...

> *in the wind,*

>> *or in the rustling of the leaves...*

> *in the sound of some unfamiliar bird calling,*

>> *or singing its sweet song to creation.*

I am always there around you,

and the message is always the same...

you are mine...

but you are free...

love does not captivate or restrict...

it cannot exist without total freedom...

and you are free...

always free...

your chains are not from me...

but from your own fear

of your reality.

Seek the truth...

    always seek the truth...

        but what is the truth of which I speak?...

        it is not found in the words of great sages...

            or in the archives of history...

                or even in the songs of angels...

        but within the darkness of your own mind...

unless you face your deepest fears,

    you cannot hear its voice...

    and when you glimpse

        that which you find most abhorrent,

        you have not found the truth...

when you feel, with great certainty,

    the scope of your own rage,

        and scorn,

            and greed,

                and lust,

                    and judgment,

                    and terror,

    you are,

        at last,

            perhaps,

                being truthful...

    but you have not reached the truth of which I speak.

That truth will announce itself, unexpectedly,
within your heart,
as warmth and compassion...
as tenderness and love...
and your tears will flow
for the entire human race...

you will feel calm and strong...
and know that my love surrounds you all...

you will realize that the degradation of the human spirit
is temporary...
and necessary...

and, although you will not permit outrageous attacks,
upon yourself,
or upon anyone else,
you will weep for the attacker,
as you weep for yourself...

and you will know, in that moment of clarity,
that it is all a part of you
and that you are all a part of me...

and that, together,
we evolve and expand...
and become what my dream consists of...
the yearning, and the unspeakable joy,
to know, for even a moment,
the meaning of our experience.

How can you know if love is present,
if you never feel the sting of hate?...

how can you respond with a generous heart,
if you never are the victims of greed?...

all is a part of the great adventure...
all is of my creation.

You fall in love with the song of the bird,
 and you would have it,
  whenever you choose...

  so you capture the bird,
   and hold it close in your delight,
    and clasp it to your bosom as your own...

   and put it in a golden cage,
    to keep it nearby,
     so that its song can thrill you...

but the bird, the poor caged creature, languishes,
 its feathers dull and drooping,
  its song silent...

 it cannot continue as itself in your grasp,
  and you lose that
   which gave you such joy...

why do you believe that I would keep you captives,
 when my joy in you
  depends upon your free expression
  and subsequent growth?

Session Twelve

Love does not depend upon the behavior of another...

    love is integral,

        and constant,

            and permeates your being...

    that which you love,

        you have glimpsed,

            in a moment of truth...

        and you are forever dedicated to its influence.

Love is not predicated upon rewards,

    or results,

        or compliance...

        it senses the spirit in essence,

            and responds with spirit in toto.

Love is seeing,
   and hearing,
      and feeling...

         and delighting in the development
            that is a part of all human interaction.

Love rejoices
   when the beloved soars to new heights
      of freedom
         and realization...

   and never binds
      with expectations
         or fear.

Love is compassion,
   and understanding...

      and a yearning to see,
         and to be seen in all your nakedness...

      and love says "no"
         when you are hidden,
            and weeps with delight
               when you are revealed.

You cannot seek to love...

> *you can only tell the truth,*
>> *which will allow love to be felt*
>> *and recognized.*

You must seek to remove the barriers to love,
> *and the barriers are pride and fear...*

> *the wish to control...*
>> *and the fear of captivity...*

>> *and, ultimately, of being controlled.*

Above all,
> *love grants freedom*
>> *to the beloved...*

and,

> *if the pursuit of truth*
>> *leads to a loved one's departure,*
>>> *love helps prepare for the venture...*

>> *and embraces the beloved,*
>> *with both its joy*
>> *and its grief,*
>>> *at the leaving.*

Love can never possess...

it can only give...

receive...

or exchange.

Session Thirteen

I do not mean to disparage the love
that you feel and experience
at any time in your life...

but only to distinguish between
what you believe to be love,
and my magnificent conception of love...

one you are experiencing in the moment...

and the other is the embodiment
of all that the word
is capable of becoming.

Nor do I wish to discourage your struggle
towards that which burns in your soul...

we would not dismiss a baby's first,
gargantuan attempts
to stand upon its feet,
on its way to running...

we would rejoice,
and applaud its efforts...

and remember, if we're lucky, how often we fell
on the way to accomplishment and success.

but when I speak of love,
I speak, specifically,
of that which I exploded into matter
with my unencompassable desire...

and I speak to open your minds...
to the grotesque distortions
that you construct...

as well as to that
which is of such power
and beauty.

Love can only be glimpsed,

when the devil of self-deception

is overcome,

for a moment...

when the spirit shines through clearly,

awakening the magnificent memory

of recognition.

"Love at first sight" is not only real,

but absolute...

for without the real sight of the beloved,

one does not love...

that moment of complete and utter exposure of the soul,

and the total connection that follows,

is vital,

if you have any hope of further progress

and understanding...

the spirits merge,

and become as one...

and all is transcended

in the ultimate peak experience.

It is eternal...

    it will prevail...

      but at great cost and upheaval...

   it is a time of total and inexplicable chaos...

    turning your world upside down...

     demanding that you place the pursuit
       of this wondrous dream
         in its proper place...

        the only goal in life worth everything...
        all that you have ever imagined...

    and crashing down upon you with this cognition...

      the terrible fear
       that to follow this path
       will cost you your soul.

From the stars into hell,

    you fluctuate at the onset of this miracle...

        to retain this treasure

            and not relinquish your spirit

                becomes your constant conflict...

    but it is only that you do not understand

        the true nature of love...

    it is only that you are so afraid

        that something so all-consuming

        and wondrous

            must have a cost

                beyond your capacity

                to pay.

Session Fourteen

The road seems so fraught with danger...
and the pain of either winning or losing
seems unbearable...

but just as you were driven to creep,
and to rise up and walk,
so are you driven to go forward
into the dark uncertainty of loving...

you have no choice...
you will learn to love...

if not this time, then the next...
or the next...
or the next...

all of you...
staggering
blindly
forward...

through the morass
of your own creation.

And there is but one road...
you cannot avoid it...

the road is truth...

the truth that you must seek out,
moment by moment...

the truth that dwells
within the deepest recesses
of your being...

the truth that you reach
after quaking in horror
at the hidden agendas
that you uncover...

and after wallowing
among your own fearful demons...

the truth that enters joyously into your heart,
as you finally recognize yourself
in everything you once detested
and feared so totally.

And, with the flowering of that truth,

compassion and tenderness replace,

for that one moment,

the rage and the rationalizing

that have blinded you to your true self...

and understanding

and acceptance

replace the fear...

and you know, for that same moment,

that when you have exposed the fear to the light,

and it has lost its power over you

by the exposure to that light,

the light of truth,

that you are all that you long to be...

and, for that brief moment,

you love...

and your deepest griefs

will reveal their exquisite beauty...

and your greatest triumphs

will be as dust.

Love cannot be bargained for...

    to bargain for love

        is solicitation...

        to seek a reward for love

           is prostitution.

When you love,

    you relinquish control...

    and the love that I speak of

        cannot be controlled...

        by even the most commanding spirit.

Listen to the voice of love...

    free and independent,

        it sings and laughs...

    in the cosmos,

        and in the innermost crevices

        of your being.

You can experience love,

but you can not hold it captive...

for it dissolves into ashes
when contained.

Truth

and beauty

and love

are one...

and there is no truth
without freedom.

You are torn at birth

from safety

and loving care,

into a strange environment,

where not even the gentlest of loving parents

can keep you safe;

you are infused with the need

to expand your horizons,

and filled with longing

to return

to your source.

Session Fifteen

You must be dedicated to but one thing,

in your present existence...

the truth...

as you find it...

to the best of your ability,

you must seek the reality that exists

at any given time...

and you have only to look,

and accept,

and uncover

what presents itself to you,

through your senses.

It is not your task to solve another's problems,

or take away another's pain...

the lessons of life

that await all who live in your dimension

are necessary,

and produce growth...

and,

therefore,

joy.

To seek the truth

with another human

is to love him...

and to accept him

if he avoids the truth

is to love him...

but to pity him

is to weaken him,

and rob him of the opportunity

that beckons him....

to help him,

with your own true responses,

to uncover that which lies hidden

is to give him the greatest gift

that you have to give...

but, at the same time,

to recognize your own wish

to escape this burdensome task

is a necessity...

and there is, within each of you,

the capacity to heal...

but without the recognition

of the disease which has created illness,

that capacity is rendered

impotent.

You pray for deliverance...
    but refuse to participate
        in the revolution that will free you...

    you wait for the appearance of a savior...
        one who will produce a miracle
            that will correct all that incapacitates you,
                without effort or commitment on your part...

    you sob out the sad refrain
        of your helplessness in the face of adversity...

        but refuse to utilize the strength
            that lies waiting to be developed
            with your sweat and tears.

No one can heal you...
    you must heal yourself...

    no one knows your truth...
        only you can uncover your self-deceptions...

        others can only speak out,
            when they cannot see you...

        when your ego has appeared,
            in one of its many guises,
                and driven you underground.

You believe that if you are loved,

    you will be protected,

        and indulged...

you know so little of love...

love knows you well,

    and when it sees a stranger in your place,

        it is love's gift to you

            to refuse to accept that imposter...

        and to warn you

        of its presence.

How foolish of you to wish for health,

    if only to continue in your charade...

for then the mind,

    which seeks truth so diligently,

will refuse to cooperate.

The opportunity that life presents is golden...

each self-deception,
exposed to the light of subjective truth,
gives wings to your spirit...

and releases you
into the moment.

Session Sixteen

You have called to me,

    in your despair...

        and you have entreated me

            to intercede in your behalf...

        I have acknowledged the pain

            that you are enduring...

        but you see only that

            which you wish removed...

you are blind to the reality

    that you are a part of...

        you are so enraged

            by my failure to return you to Eden

            that you do not realize

                that you are still in Paradise...

when, for a brief moment,

    you remove the blinders of self-deception,

        and reach the truth that resonates in your soul,

        you will be overcome

            by the beauty of that reality.

I have not condemned you only to a vale of tears,
of tragic circumstances,
and of obscenity...

you also have
the feel of the sun and the rain
upon your skin...

and the taste of honey
on your lips...

the sounds of music
that lift your soul to the heavens
with its glorious resonance...

and set your spirit free,
to dance with the wind...

the unlimited beauty that surrounds you...

sunsets that soothe your troubled mind...

the quiet and calmness of the dark,
followed by the sunrise,
bursting upon the horizon
in all its exuberance,
to begin a new day...

laughter and singing and dancing...
food and drink...
flowers and trees...
birds singing...

and each new life reminding you
of the miracle of your existence.

Session Seventeen

The gifts that have been given to you are boundless...
the world is a cornucopia of beauty and excitement...

it is all for your pleasure...
intended to be tasted...
and felt...
and heard...

it is not my intention
that you should deny yourselves anything,
from the groaning board
that is set before you...

you are exquisitely tuned to respond,
with every note on the scale
of your humanity.

It is only that you have not yet learned
how sweet the taste of honey
after the sting of salt...

or how brilliant the glorious burst of dawn
after the blackness of night...

you fear that which is light
because it is always followed by darkness...

but you do not realize
how weary your eyes would be
if that blazing light continued,
unabated...

it is the same with your emotions...

you become sated
with joy and laughter
if you do not have the contrast
of grief and pain.

You learn to see with new clarity,

and hear with renewed interest,

and long for another's touch,

when you are deprived of that

which you accept so quickly as your due...

the fresh green of spring

that stirs the heart ever anew...

laughter bubbling up from the grief-stricken soul

that had forgotten what it was to laugh...

the exquisite madness of physical love

that carries you through the bleak and lonely days

of trial and error that must follow

to reach the core of your belonging

and interwoven future...

the crashing of the waves of passion, on a rocky shore,

that wear away the sharpness,

and leave the rocks smooth to the touch,

strong and intertwined,

balancing one another, in their defense

against the tides that come and go...

always ready to sweep them away,

but cleansing them,

and cooling them,

at the same time.

Ah, the beauty,

the passion,

and the power

that are awaiting you,

and are all about you...

causing you to weep with joy,

and sending currents of electricity

through your being.

Session Eighteen

From the deepest recesses
of your being,
from that part of you
that is eternal,
comes the knowledge
that you yearn for
with such intensity.

You are surrounded, always,
    with both truth
      and deception...

  you are pulled constantly back and forth,
    between the paradise of light
      and the hell of darkness...

  this is as it was meant to be...

  you are where you are,
    at any given moment,
  in the light,
    or behind the veil,
    to remind you of your mission.

When you sink into depression,

and uncertainty,

it is to open your eyes

to your humanity,

and to remind you

of how far you have to go...

when you stumble, exhausted, into the light,

after staggering blindly, in your search,

you are comforted,

and lifted into my arms...

and you can see

how far you have come...

you feast upon the knowledge you have gained,

and rest in the shelter of my love...

you are strengthened and encouraged,

to prepare you for the inevitable conflict

that lies ahead...

you long to remain in this wondrous place...
but you see clearly that this is only an oasis
in the desert of your ignorance...

and though you may drink deeply
of its healing waters,
your journey has just begun...

your life lies ahead,
and you are meant to wander...

searching always
for the holy grail of truth...

and finding bits and pieces
of tantalizing beauty
along the way.

Session Nineteen

I am always there when you seek me...

I am within you,

and around you,

and a part of you...

there is no division that separates us...

it is only your self-deception

that closes the door...

at the core of your being,

there I am,

and in all that surrounds you,

there I am.

You are my dream incarnate...

concept and consciousness manifested...

and that consciousness is boundless,

unlimited...

capable of all that I have imagined,

and more.

You are mind,
> spirit,
>> and body...
>>> gloriously combined to evolve...

forever expanding,
> delighting me,
> and feeding my creativity,
>> as you grow.

Just as the fruit of your loins contains within it
> the seeds of all that you are,
so do you, creations of my yearning,
> contain all that I am...

each of you unique,
> but each of you identical
>> in your capacity
>>> for boundless compassion and love.

I do not control you...
> I have no limits or restrictions for you...
I rejoice
> in your growing independence and wisdom,
just as you rejoice
>> when your children cut the bonds,
> and escape the yoke of fear
>> that your parenthood
> has imposed upon them.

The clamoring passions of your humanness
propel you towards your inescapable fate...

they demand that you hear them,
and punish you with their relentless appetites,
as they lead you to dark and dangerous places,
and frighten you
with the intensity of powerful drives...

you are dashed upon the rocks of life,
and left to bleed
with the wounds
of your indiscretions.

It is not your passions
that have betrayed you...
it is your fear...

you have not determined, as yet,
how to play the marvelous instrument
that is your body,
and so you live in discordant chaos...

but you learn,
and you grow...

and you can, if you try,
discover how to use the vehicle
that you inhabit in concert
with your spirit and your mind.

You will understand
    that your failures
        are opportunities for growth...

    and that there is no growth
      without pain
        and sorrow.

There is no way
    that you can fully grasp
      the colossal concept
        which is manifested
          in the reality
            that you inhabit...

   you are limited by your humanness...

    and that humanness is responsible
      for both your pain
        and your progress.

Session Twenty

The fundamental concept is love...

it has given birth to complex thought-forms
that resonate throughout the cosmos
in a variety of ways...

but the idea of love is so beautifully simple
that it defies your comprehension...

it is all-encompassing...
and unfailing in its expression.

If you could begin to glimpse
this totality of compassion and acceptance,
you would readily lose your fears
of judgment and punishment...

there is none of either present
in the Godhead...

there is no preconceived opinion
about any given action,
at any time,
for anyone...

what it does offer, in fact,
is predicated upon
total freedom of expression.

Humanity's best

is but a pale reflection

of the incredible generosity

of acceptance...

there are not words that express

the inexpressible...

love, in its cosmic concept,

is so far removed

from even the most actualized human's

pale imitation...

and yet it infuses you

with the need to develop that concept

within the confines of your humanity...

and everything you think,

or do,

or feel,

that is the result of your passions

leads you ever towards that shining light...

and, in the process,

enhances the universal mind...

all humans,

no matter how depraved,

are driven by the same spirit force...

it is always burning within...

and the desire to know the truth

never diminishes...

it is there, beneath the fear...

the hate...

the greed...

and the cruelty

that your self-deceptions

have created.

You cannot know the nature of God in this dimension...

you can only allow the emotional force that is
to permeate your being,
and touch that part of you that is the "seed"
from which you all spring...

your common creator.

And when you examine your children,
who come from the same gene pool,
and are therefore basically alike,
and recognize the expanse
of their diversity,

you may come to realize, intuitively,
how important it is
to not only allow,
but to encourage
the uniqueness
that is your creator's joy...

and you will reject any suggestion
that there is only one path
leading to the ultimate.

Your bodies

    are meant to give you pleasure...

  the good things that abound

    are meant to be enjoyed...

  the beauty that surrounds you

    is meant to be seen...

    the emotions that are a part of you

      are meant to be felt and accepted.

Your own subjective truth

  is the holy grail that you seek...

    and there is a way

      to find that precious treasure...

  the fearless search

    for the truth of which I speak

      is the reason for life...

      you are given the lessons

        that will lead to wisdom...

you were not created man and woman by accident...

  you are meant to search together...

    and when spirit recognizes spirit,

    it opens the way to paradise.

Session Twenty-One

When the light of truth shines,

    all else falls away,

        and you are one with the universe...

            you are aware of your connection

            with all that is...

                you are a part of love...

            and you feel compassion and acceptance,

            for yourself,

                and for your fellow travelers...

    ego steps aside,

        for a brief moment,

        and you are in reality...

            at one with me,

            and aware of the eternal nature

                of your existence...

it is then that you are whole...

your spirit

and mind

at peace with your body...

both accepting it

as a necessary participant

in this experience...

judgment is momentarily suspended...

and the idea of right and wrong,

or good and bad,

falls away...

to the greater knowledge

that I am,

and that you are part of me,

and that all that transpires

is right

and productive.

But there is no final, great,

  all-encompassing truth...

    one that you will suddenly know...

      one that will release you from your journey...

  there are only brief moments

    of clarity and beauty...

      they illuminate the now,

        and they give you courage to continue...

      the light unexpectedly flashes before you,

        filling you with indescribable joy and peace...

        adding, each time, to the central premise...

          which is love,

            truth,

              and beauty.

And we all evolve...

since you crawled out of the mud,
and stood upon your two feet,
it has been thus...

the two of you,
man and woman,
urged forward by your quest...

not knowing the way,
or indeed the goal...

but driven
by the inexplicable yearning
towards creativity.

The light of truth

   becomes the fire of passion...

      to understand,

         and to be

            that which you are destined to be...

               each of you,

                  in your own time,

                     and in your own way...

               perfect in my sight...

                  everything in balance,

                     in what appears to be total chaos.

I do not lead you or guide you...

    the mind

        that is part of me

            teaches you...

    and the spirit

        that is your individual manifestation of me

            guides you.

I wait...

    when you were children,

        I spoke to you as children...

    but you are emancipated...

        and free to choose your own path

            to the reality that is my dream.

The sense of joy
and release
when the truth is unbound
is the ultimate peak experience;

at that moment,
you accept yourselves and your reality,
without censorship
or judgment.

Session Twenty-Two

"Believe not
merely because it is taught by a sage,
handed down by tradition,
or inspired by a prophet;

believe because your spirit responds,
and then believe and act accordingly."

{by an unknown author}

{altered by the psychic source}

I say to you

    that no one can tell you

        what is truth for you...

        no one can know

            which path you should take...

        no one knows

            the connection you have with me,

                or how to achieve that connection...

it is within you...

        and if you follow any other path,

        you deny your spirit...

            and that will separate you from me.

For those who believe that I control your life...
you, all of you,
create your own life,
moment by moment...

you create your own future...

you are creating it now,
as you hear my voice...

you are the product
of my mind,
and your life is the product
of your mind.

You have heard it said many times...

the future is plastic...

as indeed it is...

capable of changing...

reshaping...

renewing with great elasticity,

without breaking...

always evolving...

with each flicker of light,

you alter not only the future,

but the past as well..

bringing them together

in reality.

Only you have the ability

to create your own future...

you have no power over another...

and you have no conscious control

over the events

that you bring into your orbit...

they are the result

of your need to grow.

Session Twenty-Three

How much of your life
is based upon false premises?...
how much is distorted
by your self-deceptions?...

what connections
that you believe you have made
are real,
and therefore still valid?...

and how much
of what you believe to have happened
is fantasy,
made up to hide your failures,
and shore up a sagging ego?...

how can you know
if what you remember
is real,
or simply a dream?

Can you ever know what another feels?...

    or are you endlessly

        and hopelessly

            at the mercy of your own distortions?

Even the moment is elusive,

    and darts about,

        as if looking for an escape...

    the more you try to pin down

        the reality you seek,

            the more it tantalizes you

            with its evanescence.

Session Twenty-Four

The past is not what you believe it to be...
it is not concrete and stable...

it changes,
and reorganizes,
in much the same way
that the present does...

it is always affected by the present...
by the degree of clarity
that you are experiencing
in the moment...

and it changes forever
when you have an emotional breakthrough...

one that frees you from the fantasy
that you have created
to protect yourself
from what seemed to be
unbearable circumstances...

when, and if, such an event occurs,
 the captive that you have been in the past
  is released into the present...

  allowing that part of your personality
   to rejoin your essence, or spirit,
    that exists in and out of this dimension...

the trauma, or perceived event,
 that took you captive
  may reappear from time to time,
   to disturb you...

  but its impact
   upon your current reactions to the world
    will be less and less profound...

  and you will be able to observe the effect
   without necessarily succumbing
    to the habitual responses
     that have been directing your life
     without your knowledge
     or consent...

for all but a few of you,
 this is one of the most difficult concepts,
  not only to understand,
   but also to eventually integrate
    into your current experience.

You are capable of withstanding

any catastrophic event

when you accept

that your own response

is all that matters,

in the overall nature of things...

and that you have the strength

and courage

to endure the chaos

of reality...

that, indeed,

it is the necessary ingredient

that moves you

towards your divinity.

Your responsibility is to understand,

intellectually and emotionally,

what you have to do...

since you will continue to distort reality,

your quest is clear...

to seek these distortions

within yourselves...

to learn to view them

with interest and compassion...

to find a way

to enhance your abilities to do so...

and to rejoice

in the power of your spirit

to never fail you...

no matter how obtuse

and stubborn

you manage to be...

your essence remains constant

and uncritical...

totally committed

to your evolution.

Session Twenty-Five

You can not do this alone...

you do not evolve

by denying your humanness,

or by rejecting the pleasures of the flesh,

or by gathering together like sheep...
baaing mindlessly,
while being driven
by what you assume to be
a benevolent shepherd.

This is your world

    that we have co-created

        to teach you the secrets of the universe...

    it is meant to be experienced,

        in all its subtleties,

            and extravagances...

        until you can recognize your own truth...

        within its structure,

    and develop your own ethic,

        to propel you to the creative future,

            that you will also co-create.

You are not meant to be hermits,
or to hide away from life,
in convents of your own making...

you were meant to face life...
to be physically
and intellectually
greedy...

to partake
of all that there is...

and to take that experience with you,
when you return to the universal center...
when it is time for you to move on...

consider the prodigal son...
welcomed and feted,
without judgment
or censure,
but with joy.

It is then

that all your self-deceptions,

and distortions,

and fantasies

will be swept away...

and you will see clearly

where you have limited yourselves...

you will experience your own anguish,

and shed your own tears

of remorse and regret

at your wasted opportunities...

in the embrace

of boundless compassion,

acceptance,

and love,

you will feel everything

that you have been too afraid to feel,

and you will recognize the power

in those feelings...

you will come face to face with the demons
that have haunted
and terrorized you...

and you will recognize them
as creations of your own fears...

you will cry for those you failed to love,
and you will be cleansed by your tears...

and when you have seen clearly, at last,
the reality of your life,
you will be amazed at your progress...

grief will fall away,
and you will be eager and ready
to continue your journey,
with renewed vigor,
and a clean slate.

You had feared
that unless you were perfect,
you would not be loved...

now you will understand
that unless you are imperfect,
you are unable to love.

Session Twenty-Six

By now, you may accept the premise
that your task in life
is to ferret out your self-deceptions
and your distortions...

in order to live in the moment,
and release the creativity
that is inherently yours...

but how can you proceed in this endeavor?...

what manner of activity,
research,
or education
can facilitate this task?...

the arduous task
of returning to the essence
that is you?

I have said before

    that you are not meant to live alone...

        and it follows

            that you cannot find the true self alone...

    it is only through the eyes of another

        that you may be able to perceive yourself...

            your own view of yourself

            is always distorted.

When one "falls in love"
it is always at first sight...

that moment when,
for some inexplicable reason,
the real self is exposed to another...

in that magic moment,
when two spirits reveal themselves,
there is recognition...

and love is always present....

one could have "known" the other for years,
and never looked upon that person's soul.

Two unprotected egos,

realizing their mutual fragility

and fear...

naked, for a moment,

before one another,

and connecting totally...

love at first sight...

it may be a meeting of soul-mates,

destined to attempt again

the impossible...

or it may be only a flicker,

that dissolves almost instantly...

love is there.

Love is always there
in the presence of truth...
but all too quickly,
you hide again...

the more important another becomes,
the greater your fear...

and the more you attempt
to "be" what you think
that person will love,
and accept...

all of your doubts about yourself
are transferred to your beloved...
and you alter your behavior accordingly...

what tragedy!...

the essence is obscured
by the facade...

and that wondrous rapport
that took you to heaven
is lost in the morass
of your fear
and confusion.

Love does not die,

    or fade away,

        or degenerate into boredom,

        or tolerance...

        love is always there,

            beneath the layers of deceit

            and compromise

                that separate you from one another...

it is only the one

        who has seen the glory of your spirit

        who can recognize the stranger

            that takes over your existence...

        who can identify the alien

            that would inhabit your body...

        and who can call for the spirit to return...

the rest of the world may be enchanted

        by the persona that you have created

        to protect yourself from your fears...

        but the one who knows your real self

        will be devastated

            by the presence of an actor

            in your stead...

                no matter how skilled

                the performance.

Two of you, united,

    committed to one goal...

        the search for moment-to-moment

        subjective truth...

only you have the opportunity

    to help one another remove the debris

        that suffocates your spirit...

            and separates you...

                not only from each other,

                but from yourselves...

and, in the process,

    that first transcendent experience of love returns...

    again,

        and again...

            deeper,

                finer,

                    and calmer...

guiding you

    towards greater understanding,

        and compassion...

            for yourselves,

                and for your fellow travelers.

Session Twenty-Seven

It is all so simple...

> *and it is so difficult to achieve...*
> *the essence of life is education...*
> *and to that end, all is sacrificed.*

Look to your own relationships with your children,
and you may begin to have a glimmer
of what I am...

> *I am here, always...*
> *caring...*
> *loving...*
> *observing...*
> *waiting...*
> *and feeling the pain*
> *and confusion*
> *that you create*
> *to educate yourselves.*

And yet it is my love for you

that has taught me

that to assist you,

when you have the ability

to accomplish a task yourself,

is to weaken you...

and rob you

of the opportunity

to progress...

and that to protect you

from the consequences

of your actions

is to corrupt you...

and that to control you

is to destroy your creativity.

It was not always so...

in the beginning,
I indulged you,
protected you,
and controlled you...

I thought that I could,
by my greater wisdom and power,
propel you towards that
which I envisioned for you...

and spare you the agony
and confusion
that growth demands...

but the results were uniformly disastrous.

For you became increasingly
dependent,
    and demanding...
and, at the same time,
    rebellious,
        and self-indulgent...

you longed to be free,
    but you had no understanding
    of responsibility...

    you yearned to attempt that
    which I believed
        would bring you grief...

    and you rejected that
    which I had prepared
        so carefully for you.

My commandments,

    which were necessary

        when you were children,

        and which you originally accepted

        without question...

    seemed restrictive

    and obnoxious

        to you...

        and you became

        deceptive

        and divisive,

        in an attempt to avoid them...

    you resented my authority,

        and yet you expected my largess...

    you had no knowledge

    of love

        or creativity...

    and the beauty that surrounded you

    was unseen...

        for you knew not ugliness.

I watched these wondrous thought-forms of mine

    disintegrating

        into parasites...

I was filled with wrath

    and vengeance...

        I wished to control

            that which I had created...

        and I ranted,

          and raved,

            and punished...

have you not felt the same way,

    in response to your children's rejection?

I did not know

that love precluded

control...

I did not know

that anguish was a necessary component

of growth...

I did not know

that creations wither,

if they cannot fly into the future,

propelled by the power

of their own,

unlimited

imagination...

I had not yet learned

that the greatest gift

of love

is freedom.

Session Twenty-Eight

And so I released you
  into your own custody...

    free to find your own way...

    and liable for those errors
        which you were destined to make...

with compassion
  and love,
        I recognized the limitations
          that I had imposed
            with my guardianship...

it was time for you
  to taste the forbidden fruits
    that I had placed before you...

time for you to experiment,
  and indulge your appetites,
    in order to understand
      who
        and what
          you were...

        in all your power
        and glory
          and obscenity...

time for you to be free
  to learn
    and grow...
  in your own way,
    at your own pace...

unencumbered
  by the rules and regulations
    that would keep you safe
      but enslaved...

      that would keep you as children...
      incapable of compassion,
        understanding,
        and love.

In the beauty
and majesty
of this creation,

and in your ignorance,
and arrogance,
and pride,

you soiled your nest...
polluted the air,
the rivers,
the streams,
and the oceans,
and destroyed the majestic forests...

in your greed and lust,
you warred among yourselves...
enslaved the weak...
abused your power...
raped your women and children...
judged those who opposed you...
and laid waste to Eden...

but I would have it no other way...
for how are you to open your eyes,
your minds,
and your hearts...
and, in the process, learn?...

how are you to find,

except by your own obscene behavior,

the way to your own personal ethic?...

how will you begin to accept

the responsibility of freedom

unless you are faced

with the loss of your planet

through your own foolishness?...

how will you learn to discriminate

between that which your spirit longs for

and that which your ego craves?...

and how will you feel compassion

for those who follow you,

as they become lost in the maze

of their self-deceptions,

if you lack the personal experience?...

you have learned nothing of love

if you are "good"

because of fear of punishment

or promise of reward.

The goal is love,
and the path is truth;

that subjective truth that flickers before you,
like sunlight in a dark forest,
constantly changing,
tantalizing,

beckoning you forward,

but filling you with fear
at the awesome
darkness.

Session Twenty-Nine

As you sow,

you shall reap...

and you will learn

through bitter experience...

no one is exempt from cosmic law...

you cannot escape

the consequences of your actions...

the separation from your spirit

will leave you isolated,

and afraid...

it is only through truth,

subjective truth,

that you can find yourselves

again...

and you will...

all of you...

no matter how you struggle

to avoid the process.

And so I wait for you...

> *when you speak to me,*
> > *I answer you,*
> > > *but you do not hear me...*

I hear your pleas,
> *but I do not grant you your wishes,*
> > *like a fairy godmother...*

> *or a magician.*

I wait for your growth,
but I am here always...

when your self-deceptions
have distorted your world,
and you are bereft,
and, in terror and pain,
you turn to me,
I am here...

when you are weary,
I embrace you...

when your mind is thirsty,
you may drink
from the well of my knowledge...

and when your spirit is hungry,
you will be nourished
by the bread of life...

understanding...
compassion...
and unconditional love.

There is no judgment...
>   *you will judge yourselves...*
>>   *and in so doing,*
>>>   *you will release your spirit*
>>>   *into the now.*

The pain that you have inflicted
>   *upon others*
>   *you have inflicted*
>>   *upon yourselves...*

>   *and, someday,*
>>   *you will weep their tears,*
>>   *until*
>>>   *you are cleansed...*

>>   *and until*
>>>   *you have forgiven yourselves.*

Session Thirty

Hedonism

    is as doomed to failure

      as is puritanism...

    the pursuit of pleasure

      versus the pursuit of goodness...

      both miss the point.

The path is truth...

    there can be no other way...

    it leads you

        to your own reality...

            to your own self...

                to that which you were created for...

                ultimately,

                    it leads you to love.

And each of you is different...

    you each have your own agenda...

    you have chosen your road...

    and it is only you

        who can recognize the guideposts

        as they appear for you.

Session Thirty-One

To seek truth
    is not the way to paradise,
        it is the way to reality...

        to life,
            with all of its complications and problems...
                problems for you to address and solve...

            its turmoil and chaos...

                its fears to be faced and conquered...

                and its raging emotions...

                    grief and pain...
                    laughter and joy...
                        pleasure and beauty...

        and it is the way
            to growing wisdom,
                that will enable you
                    to fulfill your mission.

And so,

    do not live your life guardedly,

      hoping for your rewards

        in heaven...

    live your life boldly

      and honestly...

        challenging yourselves

          at every moment...

        mindful of your propensity

          to hide that which appears

           too difficult to face.

Understand your ego's need...

    to prevail,

        and to protect itself...

            recognize your fear

                in all of its disguises...

    learn to accept that

        which you have found unacceptable

        in others,

        by acknowledging

            that part of yourself

                that you deny so vehemently.

You are meant to live in the world,
   with all of its distractions
      and temptations...

         you cannot be fully creative,
            if you retreat
               from outside influences...

   it is in the actuality of interactions
      that you practice and refine
         that which you have begun to understand...

   it is through succumbing to temptation
      that you begin to differentiate
         between thought
            and action.

And just as you seek

    to accept and understand

        the forces

            that the world rejects as evil,

      recognize also that part of yourself

        that is divine,

          unlimited,

            and eternal...

                at one with the cosmic mind...

    become familiar

      with the power

        and creativity

          that your spirit possesses,

            when released from the prison

              of fear

                and self-deception...

cherish the highs

and lows

of your nature...

they enrich

and define

your being...

they allow the glorious music

of creation

to resonate...

open your minds

and hearts

to the endless possibilities

that await discovery

if you let down the barriers

that your ego has erected

to protect you...

and if you act in concert

with another who has joined you

in a mutual search

for truth.

Session Thirty-Two

Any religion,

    philosophy,

        or belief system,

            presented as truth,

      whose doctrine separates you,

         in any way,

        from any member of mankind,

            blasphemes the cosmic mind.

If you would lead another to the truth,
listen kindly
and attentively,
with an open mind...

even though the words
may seem to be
the ravings of a lunatic...

until you see yourself
in the struggling spirit
trying to extricate itself
from the web of self-deception
that the ego has woven...

then say,
"I have heard what you have said,
and you have said it well,
for I understand you...

now,
let us explore together
what is in my heart
and mind."

Session Thirty-Three

There is nothing to fear from me,
for I am love...
and that is the truth of it...

if it speaks to you
of judgment...
or fear...
or punishment...
or rules...
or regret...
or disappointment...
or rejection...
it does not come from me,
for I am love...

I do not punish...
I do not reward...
I love.

And the love of which I dream

is not conditional...

it is not influenced

by your behavior...

for your behavior

is the result of your independence,

and is the means

to your education

and growth,

and to your ultimate ability

to love,

as I love you.

The punishment you fear
comes from yourselves...
and the rewards that you anticipate so eagerly
come from yourselves...

the anguish you feel
when you look, at last,
upon the distortions of your life
is your self-inflicted punishment...

and the joy that you feel
upon escaping the bonds
of your self-deception
is reward beyond description.

I simply watch...
and wait...
and love...

and when I speak,
it is only of my glorious conception,
fulfilling itself in you.

You will come...

you will learn...

each of you will reach the goal,
and then go beyond it...

never ending...
always evolving...

creating beauty,
truth,
and love
beyond my dreams...

and I evolve with you...

for we are one.

Session Thirty-Four

Seek the truth...

and the truth shall set you free...

but what is this truth of which I speak?...

it is not factual...

although you must strive,

scrupulously,

and relentlessly,

for subjective honesty....

it is not knowledge or wisdom...

although you will acquire both

along the way...

it is not a philosophy or a religion...

although it is profoundly spiritual,

and you will develop a personal ethic

of great power and substance...

but rather, it is a state of being,

where, suddenly,

self-deception is swept away...

and you are left with the essence
of who you really are...

in that moment,

you are filled with power and glory,

and you are at one with the universe...

all fear and judgment disappear...

and what remains

is strength,

beauty,

and joy...

empathy

and compassion...

understanding

and acceptance...

and unconditional love
for all of creation...

and you will forever long to return
to this wondrous place.

If you elect to pursue this quest,
it will be as the unleashing
of tremendous forces of nature...

and you will be afraid to look at that
which you have so carefully hidden...

it will appear to strip away
the restraints of civilization,
and expose you to the terror
of your own personal demons...

it will uncover the fantasies
that you have woven
to protect your ego...

it will bring into question
every facet of your life,
no matter how cautiously,
and piously,
you have lived...

and it will shatter your illusions,
and challenge your faith.

You will look upon your piety,

your good deeds,

your noble achievements,

and your loving acts,

and you will see in them

your righteous arrogance...

your self-aggrandizement...

your vanity and pride...

your jealousy...

your wish to possess and control...

and your judgment...

always your judgment.

It will dash you upon the rocks

of your self-deception...

and leave you bloody,

and vulnerable...

but you will be free...

and you will love.

Session Thirty-Five

Do not concern yourself
with the task
of convincing others...
it does not matter
whether or not
you are believed.
{words to the channel}

What is true remains so,

regardless of the resistance of egos,

striving with all their might

to keep the bastions

that they have erected

intact.

{words to the channel}

The seed of love yearns,
as all seeds do,
to burst its bonds and produce its fruit;

it lies dormant in the darkness of ignorance,
but watered by your tears,
and exposed to the light of truth and wisdom,
it fulfills its destiny;

it is for this you are born;

it is your turn to love.

Channeling

I've had a variety of psychic experiences for as long as I can remember. Those that appeared during the first part of my life were always interesting; sometimes astounding; frequently dramatic; and occasionally very moving. They always occurred spontaneously; and, for the most part, seemed to have little practical value.

But the seeds of change were sewn almost twenty-seven years ago, when I entered into a new marriage; one where my husband and I had both committed ourselves to jointly trying to find and follow our inner truths; and one that made the two of us parents to a much larger brood, as my husband's six children were added to my five.

Both of us had always been able to handle just about anything that arose, but now we found that we sometimes felt overwhelmed. And so, at some point, whenever a particularly knotty problem arose, I began to turn to my psychic sources for help. I would deliberately try to contact them. I would relax, go into a mildly meditative state, and then present the dilemma aloud. When they responded, I would "hear" their words; and, as I spoke them, my husband would write them down, either by hand, or on a typewriter.

We consistently were given guidance and counseling of great worth; advice that, more often than not, we did not want to hear (at least at the moment); and, despite our reluctance, our education proceeded.

From time to time, I also acted as an intermediary of sorts. A friend or a member of the family would want help, and would ask me to contact my psychic sources. When I agreed to do so, we would follow the same procedure, with similar results.

After receiving countless valuable messages from these sources over many years, I began to feel less of a need for their help, and finally reached the point where I only occasionally turned to them in this way.

The circumstances that led to this book, and the process by which it came into being (the particular form of "channeling" that was used), are quite different.

A number of months ago, I began to feel pushed to collect some of the more interesting messages that we had received over the years, and place them in a book. As we sifted through the many papers, looking for the "gems," we came across several very unusual typewritten pages, from about twenty years ago, and we were struck by their wisdom and beauty.

We remembered that they had not been produced in the same way as the other material, and we decided to try that approach again. We were so moved by the results that we abandoned, for the time, our earlier idea, and, encouraged by my psychic sources, concentrated instead on producing this book (where those early sessions became the opening pages).

Behind each "session" of this book is a concept. What I mean by "concept" is extremely hard for me to explain, because whatever I'm about to receive is not given to me in words. It is very real and clear to me, however, and I understand it on a primal, non-verbal level. I compare it to the way a baby understands its mother's devotion to him. That is a very complex and intricate idea, but one for which he has no words, as yet, to use in describing it.

A concept can come into my mind at any time, and I'm always aware that it's happening. I was introduced to some just before a session began; but others had germinated in previous weeks, or months, or even years, and then had evidently been "stored" in my subconscious.

In fact, I received many of them during one concentrated period over twenty years ago. At that time, I experienced what was, to me, a profoundly spiritual experience... an "altered state"... that lasted about three weeks. During that time, many concepts were presented to me in a very rapid and constant stream; I was inundated with them. I "knew" that I would not remember all of them, although I desperately wanted to.

A few did stay in my conscious mind; but more of them seemed to be deposited at a deeper level. Over the years, usually as the result of a stimulus, one would surface, and then I would remember, with great clarity, the initial introduction.

Whenever a concept is being prepared for transmission, I have dreams that condition my thinking (for want of a better explanation). I find it very difficult to sleep at night, and I'm strangely restless during the day. This may go on for several hours, or it may last for days, or even weeks.

After a while, the restlessness disappears. The new ideas and information have been integrated into my consciousness, and I feel very positive; light and calm; even joyous.

At this point, I have a strong, persistent urge to go to the keyboard, and when I do, the channeling process begins. I use a portable computer with the screen turned off. I get into a relaxed, comfortable, "meditative" state, and then I wait. In a few minutes, my hands will begin to type.

What comes through may, indeed, be an "old" or a "new" concept, and may even be one that I have in mind. Then again, it may be on an entirely different subject; something that had been processed at another time; perhaps from that brief period of many years ago.

So, sometimes I do have a general awareness of what the concept being verbalized is about, but I never have any idea of the words that are being used to express it. In fact, any time that I begin with words in my mind... words that I'm sure are about to be typed... I am inevitably wrong, for a totally different subject will always be addressed.

When the typing starts, the letters come through rapidly, in a rhythmic, almost hypnotic, constant stream; a completely automatic process, with no punctuation or capitalization, with phonetic spelling, and with plenty of typographical errors (I'm a very poor typist). But in any event, I am, almost always, completely unaware of the words themselves.

If I've made an error in the text... used the wrong word, for instance... the flow will stop. I will sit and wait for a correction, not knowing what is about to be changed. Most of the time, the replacement word, or words, will emerge, and the flow will then continue. If, however, I get it wrong again, the source will stop, and refuse to go on.

If I appear to be blocked, I'm apt to receive helpful hints and instructions, which I do read. They come through me in the original way, and I'm aware of what's being said.

At some point, the typing will abruptly stop; sometimes as much as an hour or so after I have begun, or occasionally after I have only received a line or two, even after days of restlessness.

I do not, except in rare and isolated instances, read what I have received after the typing has stopped, and I have no idea of how the concept has been expressed. I wait, at least until my husband has cleaned up the mess of my typing, and finished the task of arranging the material. He does not, in any way, change the text, the words, the ideas, or the order.

When, at last, I read what has been channeled, I am seeing it for the first time. I read it intuitively, rather than logically, at first; checking for jarring notes, to see if some word or phrase says "no" to me, indicating that I may have made a mistake in transmitting. In that case, I go back to the computer. I change nothing on my own.

Then I read it for understanding, and I find that I have absolutely no sense of authorship. In fact, I am consistently surprised; and always overwhelmed, overcome with emotion, and moved to tears. And the more I re-read any of the material, the further removed I feel from involvement in the process that created it, and the more emotionally I respond to the text.

I know that I did not write this book. I know that I simply acted as a conduit for the messages, which were transmitted from some unknown source, in an amazingly short amount of time. The whole process... thirty-odd sessions, each one lasting thirty to sixty minutes... took place over approximately a two month period.

I make no assertions about either the origin or the meaning of this material. It is simply presented as I have received it. I do have my opinions, of course, but I realize that what I believe to be true for myself may or may not be true for anyone else. As the sessions themselves make perfectly clear, each one of us is free to make our own choices, and to draw our own conclusions.

Epilogue

When my wife and I first met, we approached each other slowly and cautiously... (even though the mutual attraction was nearly overpowering)... because both of us had made our full share of mistakes... and both of us had lived long enough to realize just how difficult it was to establish and maintain a good relationship. And so we talked... for hours, and days, and weeks, and months... exploring... questioning... and explaining... and eventually covering just about every subject that interested or intrigued either or both of us... a process that was frequently energizing... but sometimes enervating... and frustrating.

During that time, both of us also started to expose our innermost selves to the other... to disclose secret successes and failures... as well as hidden hopes and fears... to reveal private likes and dislikes... along with undeclared loves and hatreds... all very naturally... all with no goal or purpose in mind. But the heady and uplifting feelings... of ease... of total acceptance... of mental intimacy... of "connection"... that almost always ensued contrived to lure us on... to push us to do more of the same.

Finally, belatedly, we became fully conscious of exactly what was happening to us... we realized that we reveled in not having to walk on eggs... in not having to pretend... and so we decided to take matters into our own hands. We resolved to try to be completely honest with each other... to expose (although usually with great reluctance) those things about ourselves that we'd much rather leave concealed... matters from both the past and the present... whether they were words or deeds... or feelings or thoughts... particularly, and most troublesome, any and all negatives that we found ourselves harboring toward the other.

Such was our unwitting introduction to the previously unheard-of concept of "subjective truth"... such were our first tentative and uncertain steps upon the unusual road that was to become our life's "work"... our primary path... indeed, our only path... one that we have diligently, if erratically, struggled to follow for more than a quarter of a century now... (despite the enormous obstacles)... one that quickly became the final arbiter of all our choices and conflicts... and one that continues to lead us onward... and, as we hope and generally believe, upward.

But this notion of inner truth proved to be unexpectedly strange and complex... by no means as obvious and simple as we had naively imagined... and the search took us down previously unseen byways... into alien and unrecognizable territories... and usually dragged us over very difficult and dangerous ground.

Despite these serious drawbacks, the often surprising but always welcome rewards insistently drove us forward... and also inevitably increased our commitment to this path... one that we acknowledge to be very much out of the ordinary.

We don't believe that words alone can provide a full and satisfactory description of the majority of those rewards... we think that they have to be felt... that they must be experienced... that only then can they be wholly and accurately understood.

But one reward... if we can call it that... one that may transcend all the others... can be fairly easily described. Our twenty-seven-year-long pursuit (thus far) of inner truth has insistently led us to form an unusual and often unsettling picture of ourselves... and, or so we believe, of the entire human race.

That description challenges almost every view we have of ourselves... almost every opinion we might possess of what's behind any of our feelings or thoughts or words or deeds. In fact, we now think that we usually know next to nothing about what's going on inside of us... that what we believe to be true about our motivation at any moment is almost always grossly distorted... and that we're burdened, each and every day, with an unseen host of unpleasant consequences of those distortions.

But we're not left dangling helplessly, with nowhere to turn... for that picture also provides a very unusual but quite simple description of what we're really like... of why we think and feel and speak and act as we do... (a point of view that most of us would probably choose to dispute or ignore).

And, by using this information, we understand how we can overcome the self-deceptions that always arise out of our distorted view of ourselves... we're familiar with the difficulties and pitfalls we may encounter, if we choose to take that route... and we're well aware of what the rewards can be. Finally, and perhaps most important of all, we believe we have more than a glimmer of what this exercise we call "life" is really all about.

Curiously, we think that an intimate relationship with a spouse (or a mate) is an absolute prerequisite to successfully exposing our self-deceptions and finding our subjective truths... and that, conversely, exposing our self-deceptions and finding our subjective truths is an absolute prerequisite to a successful intimate relationship with a spouse (or a mate).

That is, to us, the whole business is circular... we believe that the only effective way to consistently find one's subjective truths is through an intimate relationship with a mate... and that the only effective way to achieve an intimate relationship with a mate is by consistently finding one's subjective truths.

Our long journey and its accompanying education would undoubtedly have been considerably more difficult were it not for my wife's extraordinary psychic abilities. When we set out together on the road to subjective truth, we were completely on our own... we had no suggestions or help of any sort... but after we'd been at it for a few years, we began to deliberately seek contact... and were repeatedly rewarded with pointed messages pertaining to our quest... and we now believe, with no question whatsoever, that this help was forthcoming only because of the strange road we'd chosen to travel.

The interest of our psychic source was usually limited to matters of ethics, morality, spirituality, and philosophy... and its attention was consequently focused on our attitudes... our words... and our actions. In speaking to us, it encouraged... advised... and informed... and, all too often, but justifiably so, it chastised.

From our present vantage point, I firmly believe that our progress would have been far, far less were it not for this most unusual assistance... and we seem to have acquired the basics of an extraordinary education... through a combination of our own efforts and those of our unearthly guides.

Now, as we contemplate the endless path that lies ahead of us... the difference between our comparative adolescence and the god-like maturity that will, unfortunately, forever elude us... we're most thankful that our "gurus" still continue, from time to time, to inform, advise, and encourage... and we even appreciate being chastised... although generally not until well after the fact.

To go one step further, let me mention that this particular psychic source has repeatedly stated that my wife and I have always been destined to meet... to happen upon the concept of subjective truth... and to choose to pursue it together... in order (hopefully) to acquire some very special and extremely valuable information and understanding... and then to write about what we believed we had learned... and about how we had learned it... (although that same guide has often stressed that we were, in no way, compelled to take those difficult steps).

In other words, the two of us were slated to be nothing more or less than agents... or conduits... solely for the ultimate benefit, we suppose, of any and all who might be interested.

That whole idea might be difficult for many to swallow... perhaps even for me... but it's fascinating... whether true or not.

The sessions have not stopped... far from it... although those with the entity that wrote the words in this book do seem to be over.... at least for the time being. In their place, we've had a number of "meetings" with a rather different source... which, incredibly, appears to be identifying itself as Christ... at least, according to our interpretation of the material.

Some of this covers much the same ground as a few of the messages from the first source... about why we're here... and where we go wrong. But it also chastises the faithful of the world for their gross distortions of the meaning of what Christ had to say... and then includes... as did the first source... brief, beautiful, poetic phrases that inform and inspire.

If this material continues to flow... and we have reason to expect that it will... and if the content and quality remain at their current impressive level, we hope that we'll have the will and the energy to incorporate these sessions into another book... in the not-too-distant future.

We also may put into book form... sometime... a collection of the pertinent messages from our more human source... the one that calls itself "Mama." These cover much of the same ground as do the first two... although they're not as well organized... (since they appeared in bits and pieces over many years... in response to our struggles)... but they do it in much more detail... in far greater length... and they range into other, quite different areas... some of which are very intriguing... and, while generally well-written, they're not nearly as poetic... in fact, they're much more prosaic.

We've actively and deliberately pursued subjective truth together for more than a quarter-century now... and we think that we have a fairly good grasp of most of what our psychic sources are saying to the world... and we certainly have no quarrel with any of it. But they seem to have done little more than hint at what might be the most important subject of all... at least for humans on this planet... and that's the difficult business of delving into the down and dirty... of unequivocally describing the nitty-gritty of self-deception and subjective truth.

And so we think it may be left to us to try to do this job... to someday write a short book that offers our view of the more practical aspects of the matter... but to go into enough detail to convey that picture clearly... including how we think it can best be pursued... what serious problems we've encountered along the way... what rewards we've managed to glimpse... and what practical and metaphysical questions we think it answers... (all in all, a daunting task).

And a final note... in talking about our search, we hope we haven't given the impression that we think we've reached the mountain top... for nothing could be further from the truth. On the contrary, we sometimes look ahead and see how impossibly far we have yet to travel... and we're dismayed by the infinite gap between what we actually are and what we theoretically could be. But when we look back, we clearly see the enormous strides we've made... and we believe, without question, that it's all been worthwhile.

And so the search goes on... and on... and on...